What To Do When Your Kid Is Smarter Than You

A Practical Guide for
Parents, Grandparents, Teachers and Friends
on Taming and Surviving the Gifted, Talented,
Terrifying or just Terrific Kid

by
Linda Levitt

If you are a parent so exhausted by your child that you find yourself, in your pajamas, at 6:00 AM, dropping your child off at school or day care the VERY MOMENT that the doors open...

Or perhaps, as the parent of a 13-year-old, who, even though he has lost two cell phone handsets, has gone over his minutes by hundreds of dollars each month, has been busted for text-messaging his girlfriend in geometry class, and who does NOT even attempt to earn an allowance...you find yourself in line at T-Mobile having been convinced by him that you need to buy yet an even BETTER and more advanced cell phone...

Then, this book is for you!

If your child has already worn you out, and you are years away from downloading college applications... read on.

You are not alone.

You Know You're In Trouble When...

You wake up in the middle of the night, nose to nose with your child's small face, and he asks you if that money you put into the bank each Friday, instead of buying him toys, says "FOR COLLEGE ONLY" on the account? He's asking you this, he says, because if you die, he's NOT going to college. He already hates Preschool!

On the first day of kindergarten your brilliant and beloved five-year old comes running out of the classroom to greet you with the shout of "You lied! You lied! You said school was going to be fun and it was NOT! All we did was sit, sit, sit, then she yelled, yelled, yelled and I'm never, never, never going back, back, back!"

Your child gets off the bus after the first day of school and comes running to greet you shouting, "You are going to LOVE this school, Mom! They are NEVER going to call and complain about me! I'm NOT the bossiest kid in the class! You should meet Nick! I'm not even the loudest, or the noisiest, or the most annoying! Well…I'm probably still the most annoying!"

The MADHouse summer camp director calls to tell you that your child cannot be in the play because he doesn't know his lines. You are informed that he will be relegated to "The Nerd" in the crowd scenes. During the play, when every other child forgets their lines, your child calmly prompts them from his prone position on the corner of the stage. When questioned as to why he had not said HIS part during practices when he knew the whole play, he replies quietly, "I just didn't want them to hear me so I was saying the words under my breath."

You Know You're In Trouble When...

On a daily basis, when dressing himself, your child puts EVERY SINGLE ITEM of clothing on inside out or backwards, including a hooded sweatshirt...and he/she is ten years old.

Your child is chosen to take the qualifying test for the Gifted and Talented Program in your school district and he crosses out with a big "X" and puts a question mark on many of the items explaining that, "I marked out the ones I wasn't ABSOLUTELY sure of. If this is a test for SMART kids, I don't want them to think I'm dumb by marking the wrong answer."

Or even worse, your child is chosen to take the qualifying test for the Gifted and Talented Program in your school district and is finished in less than time than it took the proctor to give the directions. When it is suggested that he/she "check over his answers," he replies witheringly, "Smart kids don't have to think...they just know."

When asked what he'd do if he had Three Magical Wishes, your six-year-old is quite clear in his answers, He says that first, he would ask for totally, unlimited wishes, second, for totally, unlimited gold. And, third, he adds with a sigh, he would ask for the invention of an easier-to-use cell phone for his mom!

This book is dedicated to my two sons,
Brian & Tad, terrific kids...

Forever and always.

What To Do When Your Kid Is Smarter Than You

by
Linda Levitt

Yahoo!

Your kid is a terrific kid, too!

Look at it this way...
The journey with your child is so short
in the time frame of your whole life.

I thought of how much I'll miss my sons when they're older and have
moved out, as I snapped at my youngest yesterday, telling him to
stop making "goofy kid-noises" in the car. He rolled his eyes
and said, "Oh, gee, Mom, do you want me to start making
grown-up noises? Let's see, 'Oh, my aching neck...moan, moan...
not another bill...&^%#%...DID YOU BRUSH YOUR TEETH?...
Do I look really old and wrinkled?...
cough, cough...Go do something you HATE! It builds character!'"
I nearly drove off the road laughing.

Look for the joy.
Take a deep breath.
Grab a pen.
Uncap a highlighter...
and read on.

Introduction

I'd like to introduce myself, add some credibility to the ideas and suggestions I've compiled in writing this book.

I am a 53-year-old woman, with four children still living in my home. Oh, OK, I admit it. At this time my 16-year-old son has chosen to spend most of his time at his dad's house since he's not happy with my stricter parenting style. But I am hopeful that his perception will alter since I miss him a lot. And, he was the catalyst who turned my interest toward gifted education.

I have recently retired. I've spent the last 30 years teaching school in a variety of areas of regular education and special education, specializing in exceptional learners. After the birth of my afore-mentioned oldest son, I began to explore the needs of gifted children. Through him, I discovered the joys of working with kids who were smarter than me!

I have read hundreds of teacher's manuals, parental self-help books and attended workshops on child-rearing practices all over the USA. I've also dealt with my share of teachers, parents, coaches and judges begging them to give my children just one more chance.

Last year I formed a consulting company, Educating Exceptional Learners, and wrote this book to remind myself that, regardless of where my own children are on their life path, I know the dynamics and the "how to" of parenting kids appropriately. I am offering guidance, advice and a humorous perspective to parents and friends of our younger inhabitants of this planet…"terrific children."

Being a parent has completely altered my view of life and educational practices and adjusted my thinking on how to encourage kids to learn. I've

Linda Levitt

met many parents, who, like me, are befuddled by their bright offspring and who are actively searching for and seeking support to make the best of the time they have together.

Every day I struggle with the demands of parenting.

I am in awe of and blessed with smart children.

I am just like you.

Changes in Children and Childrearing

If you were a kid any time in the last forty years, or if you've been raising kids during the last forty years, then you know that children are MUCH different today than they were in the past.

Whether this is the result of a hole in the ozone, the replacement of real food with fast food as our primary diet, the changes in the structure of the nuclear family, the demise of the rural lifestyle, the overwhelming placement of modern technology as the centerpiece of our daily lives, or easy access for most of the population to mind-altering substances is debatable. These environmental and familial influences are here to stay and more are on the way.

The end result is that today, parenting successful children is much different and much more complicated than it was in the 1950's. It has become extremely challenging for even the most well-equipped and well-intentioned.

Children now live in a multitude of family styles and arrangements. We have one-parent, stepparent, same gender parent and too-busy parent families. Discipline beliefs and strategies are vastly different among many parents and adults, often within the same home. Communities have an endless variety of school choices and educational models to weigh and measure as we choose what is best for our children.

Linda Levitt

Some kids are too busy; some are not busy enough. Children have to be constantly entertained because there really isn't satisfying, necessary and important work that must be done in many of their own homes to sustain the lifestyle they lead with their families.

Too many hours are spent with non-interactive technology—TV, videos, computers—or, even worse, inappropriate TV, videos and computer games. Or expensive but unsatisfying toys clutter their rooms and often lead to boredom and acting-out behavior.

Most families don't have all the answers. Terrific kids can create terrific problems. And unless you have "a village" to help you raise your child, it's hard to find support.

When your child becomes unmanageable, you become exhausted or the school expresses concern, a variety of medical doctors, therapists and psychologists are available, at great expense, to diagnose, advise and offer services or medication for all sorts of childhood behaviors of today. Being sent to the principal's office, waiting until Dad gets home, a good spanking, or going to Grampa's farm for the summer just aren't universal options anymore.

HOW TO RUIN YOUR TERRIFIC CHILD IN TWELVE EASY STEPS

1. ALWAYS have to be right. Make certain your child knows YOU are much smarter than they are.

2. Stay in CONTROL of your child's life as much as you possible can! Boss them around! Save them from every mistakes or incorrect decision!

3. CRITICIZE your child at every possible opportunity — their hair, clothes, grades, friends, ideas, interests!

4. Expect your child to be PERFECT! Never settle for SECOND BEST!

5. Make sure your child knows THEIR BEHAVIOR EMBARRASSES you and the family. Tell them often and in front of other people

6. Fill your home with conflict and disagreement over parenting and child-rearing practices.

7. Expect order, organization and cleanliness from your child at all times.

8. Don't praise your child. It might spoil them.

9. Hang on to every word your child utters. Photograph every move. Make certain your child's every wish and demand is met.

10. TV, video games and computers make great baby-sitters. Sit your child in front of one as often as possible.

11. Say "SHHH" and "BE QUIET" a hundred times a day.

12. Use the phrase "BECAUSE I SAID SO" as your primary form of decision-making.

Linda Levitt

Behavior Modification

Changing Behaviors

THE "ABC" MODEL OF BEHAVIOR ANTECEDENT - BEHAVIOR- CONSEQUENCE

A firm understanding of basic behavior management is crucial if you want to understand your child's behavior. Your child already understands this model and has been using these same strategies to manipulate you! It's pretty simple.

A "BEHAVIOR" is something that is observable and measurable. You can see it or hear it....like watching your child cut off the last of her hair because "it was bugging her" or listening to your son madly blowing bubbles through a straw stuck into his BIG GULP telling you he is "pretending it is Osama Bin Laden sizzling in Hell."

Behavior does not exist in a vacuum. BEHAVIOR (something observable) begins with an ANTECEDENT (what happens before). BEHAVIOR is followed by a CONSEQUENCE (what happens after the behavior).

As parents and caregivers, we can observe, analyze, change and attempt to control the ANTECEDENT and the CONSEQUENCE in an attempt to alter the BEHAVIOR. We work with what happens before or after.

EXAMPLE:

BEHAVIOR

As you are shopping in your favorite upscale grocery store, your child begins to whine and pull items off the shelves.

ANTECEDENT

You can alter the antecedent.

1) the stores you choose to take your child in,

2) the admonitions you whisper in their little ears before you sweep through the automatic doorway,

3) or how tight a grip you have on their nimble fingers.

CONSEQUENCE

OR, you can alter the consequence:

1) what you say to them in your nicest parental voice as they dismantle the advertising kiosk for canned ham,

2) what sticky treat you tell them they will get to buy from the candy aisle at the end of this bonding experience if they immediately replace each item, or

3) how fast you carry them kicking and screaming out of the store .

Linda Levitt

YOU ARE THE PARENT!

You are in control of the antecedents and consequences in much of your child's daily life and you can change them in an attempt to change behavior.

When inappropriate behavior occurs, analyze what happened in their environment that allowed the behavior, and alter the "before" or "after".

You don't always have to resort to punishment or "time outs". Subtle and careful manipulation and rearrangement of the variables can give parents the edge.

KEY POINT: WHEN CHANGING BEHAVIOR YOU MUST REPLACE (THE UNWANTED) BEHAVIOR WITH ANOTHER (MORE DESIRABLE) BEHAVIOR.

Try this approach instead:

EXAMPLE:

BEHAVIOR

Holding your child's hand slightly tighter, together you sweep through the automatic doorway of your favorite upscale grocery store.

ANTECEDENT

In the parking lot, you have already whispered in their little ears that they may pick out ONE sticky treat from the candy aisle as a reward for quietly helping you find items in the store while they keep one hand on the cart at all times or you will be leaving immediately

CONSEQUENCE

Anticipating a treat while being busy and helpful, your chid has helped you painlessly purchase one week's groceries while learning to read labels, compare brands, keep a running tally of your spending and build muscles by pushing a two-ton shopping cart! So, you happily buy them WHATEVER they choose from the candy aisle with a smile, a handshake and the cheery deserved praise of "Thank you. Job well done!"

TERRIFIC KIDS TAKE ON THE "ABC MODEL OF BEHAVIOR" ANTECEDENT - BEHAVIOR- CONSEQUENCE

Bright children are awesome manipulators. They are often intuitive, observant, and pretty quick at figuring things out, especially when it pertains to getting what they want.

Even at a very young age, they have a view of how things should be and how to get it. They have already figured out how to jockey with the antecedents and are willing to live through, go around or ignore many of the consequences we hand out in order to behave in the way they choose!

The same ABC Model of Behavior mentioned in the previous pages still applies to terrific kids. BUT...

You just have to be prepared to outthink them, outsmart them, or out-last them!

Terrific kids often manage our behavior by a model that looks like this.

Bright children:

1) MANIPULATE the antecedent

They mentally plan in advance, think past you, are very prepared to get what they want no matter what it takes.

2) ANTICIPATE the consequences

They have thought about what you are going to say or do, and already know what could happen. Having already thought through it, they have an argument for everything. They are going to try to wear you down.

3) EMPATHIZE with the behavior – yours and theirs

They often have the ability to walk in your mind, get in your shoes. They intuitively know what you are trying to get them to do or not to do and have a better plan.

Their intelligent analysis of situations makes them pretty tricky to manage and requires us to work much harder at choosing catchy antecedents and consequences if we want to alter their behaviors.

Linda Levitt

Labels

Linda Levitt

"ADHD?"
"GIFTED?"
"TALENTED?"
OR
"TERRIFIC?"

Linda Levitt

"ADHD?" "GIFTED?" "TALENTED?" OR "TERRIFIC?"

There are many different labels and terminologies being used today to describe terrific children. Your child probably fits into one category...or several. Smart children are sometimes referred to as "gifted," "talented," "creative," "a genius," "super smart," or "precocious." Or, sometimes less pleasantly, terrific kids are referred to as "A Little Know-it All," " Too Big For Their Britches," "Difficult," "Lazy," "ADHD," an "Indigo Child," a "Problem in Class," or a "Completely Spoiled Brat."

Terrific children are often misdiagnosed. Their brightness manifests itself in other ways that often don't seem very bright. AND, no matter what the label, many of the characteristics and behaviors that concern parents and educators exist to some degree in all terrific children.

Children are often assigned labels to explain their behaviors, some of which are invented and coined to get support services in school. These labels can be right on, a partial answer, or totally erroneous but might be used to help parents join the correct parent group or to expedite the typing in of the right verbiage in a search engine when looking for information to help their child.

Checklists, observations and tests are used by parents, schools, psychologists and other experts in an attempt to categorize and label a variety of behaviors exhibited by children. There are many web sites with great information about gifted and talented and terrific children. A list of the best is at the back of this book. Check it out.

Sometimes these labels help us understand our children better. Sometimes labels such as "gifted" are used to place students in academic programs in schools and communities and are often determined by test scores. Gifted tests and testing guidelines and definitions vary in each state.

To complicate matters further, qualifications for various programs differ within each school district and within each state. This information can often be

Linda Levitt

found on the web sites for the Department of Education for your state and/or on the school district's web page or at the Special Service department of your school district's office.

Your child is a terrific child, wonderful and unique in many ways, and to you, a gift. Your child may have unusual talents or behaviors, have intense interests or skills, or simply be confounding you with all that they know and with what they want or need to do. Being referred to by various family members or professionals as gifted or talented, precocious or creative, an Indigo child, ADHD, or a CSB doesn't change their behavior or help you deal with them.

What does matter is your interest in enjoying them, guiding them, in how you choose to capture their essence, in supporting them and, ultimately, in surviving them.

If your school or community provides special programs designated specifically for terrific, talented and gifted youth, seek them out. If they require testing or test scores for your child to receive services, then by all means, accept the testing offered by your public school or seek out private testing. If you child does not qualify, but you feel they are truly gifted, don't give up. Pursue alternate ways to allow your child to participate in challenging, innovative programs. You can continue to advocate for your child's education by showcasing your terrific child in ways other than test scores. Some programs are flexible enough to consider portfolios of children's work. Some even allow written observations by teachers, or a trial period of acceptance into a program. Of course, your offer of volunteering to help never hurts.

Another avenue is to seek out programs on-line in fields of "terrific-ness." You can join programs in the arts, in athletics, or in science and math in your community that are designed for and seeking interested participants and terrific kids.

WHICH CHILD IS YOUR CHILD?

"THE OUTSMARTER"
When denied a Happy Meal your child says,
"I'm gonna cry until YOU cry!"

"THE KID ON OVERDRIVE"
After the first weeks of preschool, the teacher hands you a pile of blank
accident reports and asks you to sign them in advance saying that she can't
possibly contact you every time your child gets injured AND teach, too!

"THE HUMAN SEARCH ENGINE"
Your ten year old says that he/she knows he wants to go to college to
be an engineer, but can he also take art classes and architecture classes
and geology classes and play the trumpet, football and lacrosse?

"THE FUNNY, FUNKY KID"
Your child's can be found wandering around the backyard in their favorite
outfit — stark naked except for an orange bandanna tied pirate
style around their head and a pair of cowboy boots.

"THE PERFECTIONIST"
After three failed attempts to create the perfect Mother's Day card,
your child rips the carefully colored papers into a jillion tiny squares,
and drops them slowly, sadly in the garbage can.

Linda Levitt

COMMONLY IDENTIFIED
CHARACTERISTICS OF TERRIFIC KIDS

Advanced Vocabulary

Constantly Questioning

Curious

Creative

Demanding of Justice and Fairness

Easily Bored

High Energy

Intense

Imaginative

Insightful into Cause and Effect Relationships

Keen Observer

Leadership

Out of Sync

Perfectionist

Problem-Solver

Procrastinates

Quick Mastery and Recall of Factual Information

Rapid Learner

Sense of Humor

Storehouse of Information

Uninhibited, Independent, Non-Conforming

CLEVERLY CATEGORIZED
CHARACTERISTICS OF TERRIFIC KIDS

"THE OUT SMARTER"
HIGHLY VERBAL CHILD

Advanced Vocabulary	Keen Observer
Constantly Questioning	Problem-Solver
Demands Justice and Fairness	Insightful

"KID ON OVERDRIVE"
VERY ACTIVE KID

Curious	Imaginative
Easily Bored	High Energy

"THE HUMAN SEARCH ENGINE"
MILLION INTERESTS KID

Curious	Rapid Learner
Intensity/Passion/Focus	Storehouse of Information
Out-of-Sync	Quick Mastery of Facts

"THE FUNNY, FUNKY KID"
UNINHIBITED, AMUSING NONCONFORMIST

Sense of Humor	Creative
Uninhibited, Independent	Non-Conforming

"IT HAS TO BE RIGHT, I HAVE TO BE RIGHT"
PERFECTIONIST

Creativity	Leadership
Procrastination	Intensity

Linda Levitt

"THE OUTSMARTER"

THE HIGHLY VERBAL KID

Linda Levitt

"THE OUTSMARTER"
THE HIGHLY VERBAL KID

As many terrific kids are able to do, my son taught himself to read at a very young age. He read voraciously. At about age eight he asked me why everyone was beginning to die in his books? We discussed that, since he was reading books for older kids, stories were beginning to deal with real life, and that authors were more likely to write books that were sadder.

Before I could launch into any of my motherly advice on life, he announced that reading wasn't safe for him anymore because even the HARDY BOYS characters were dying off! I told him that was ridiculous! That NOBODY died in Nancy Drew or Hardy Boys series.

In the dark, his little voice immediately began to contradict me as he proceeded to spout off a "scene" from one Hardy Boys mystery he'd finished reading. He quoted from memory for about 10 minutes, "the yellow coupe careened around the corner as Joe swung the wheel frantically trying to narrow the space between them and the escaping bandits...a shot rang out!"

On and on he went until I was laughing so hard I had to stop him and ask WHY in the world had he memorized a Hardy Boy's book?

" Well, I choose to memorize what I find interesting," he replied nonchalantly, "I just liked the way the words flowed through my head."

Linda Levitt

#6 NOTES ON THE OUTSMARTER #9

CHARACTERISTICS OF

"THE OUTSMARTER"

Their favorite T-shirt- "Not LARGE, but IN-CHARGE"

- LOVES to argue

- Talks early, has a very advanced vocabulary

- Excellent Memory

- Keen observer of life

- A Problem Solver

- Constantly questioning

- Demands justice and fairness

- Has uncanny insight into cause and effect

- Wants reasons behind the rules

- Loves logical activities like working with money, calendars, puzzles

- Plays elaborate, complex, challenging games

- Enjoys older friends and activities for older children because they like to match wits with them

- Comes up with new ideas and applies them in innovative and creative ways

Linda Levitt

"THE OUTSMARTER"

"I've decided what I'll be when I grow up," said the three year old, "I'll be a banker and own a bank. Then I'll have all the money we'll ever need."

GOOD NEWS ABOUT THE HIGHLY VERBAL KID

- The bright brain is a really marvelous gift and provides the opportunity for an interesting life.

- Terrific kids learn really fast.

- Advanced vocabulary allows for interesting conversation at a very young age.

- The interests and perspectives of children are refreshing to hear.

- Matching wits with them will help keep YOUR brain young.

- They remember EVERYTHING, so you don't have to.

- The world can only benefit from seekers of true justice.

- They are often really good with technology and can help you figure out your cell phone, DVD player and remote devices.

- They are lots of fun to play games with…as long as they win!

- Creative problem-solvers will salvage our world.

"THE OUTSMARTER"

"Mommy, I've been thinking. I always thought I was going to marry you when I grew up. But I just counted and when I'm old enough to get married... you're gonna be dead!"

BAD NEWS ABOUT THE HIGHLY VERBAL KID

- They question EVERYTHING.

- Then, they argue with your responses.

- They ask you questions they already know the answer to just to trick you into extended discussions.

- Negotiating with a child about <u>everything</u> is exhausting.

- Their observations about many things are insightful...but can be embarrassing.

- "No" just never cuts it; they have to know "Why?"

- They are capable of manipulating you before you are aware of their long-range plans.

- Arguing in public bothers other people.

- They may have difficulty with authority, or anyone who dares to disagree with their perspective.

- They'll *do* just about anything to win.

- Friends and interests are often out-of-sync with their age.

Linda Levitt

WHAT YOU CAN DO TO SUPPORT
THE "OUTSMARTER"

1. Be prepared and be patient. Allow time for your child to "discuss" with you many important issues and questions in their lives.

2. Encourage, enhance and expand their vocabularies and interests by including them in many activities and conversations. Don't speak "down" to them.

3. Provide lots of games and opportunities where reasoning, deduction and logic are the focus. There are many old-fashioned word games, card games and board games that need to be resurrected as well as new educational toys and games for terrific kids.

4. Let yourself be challenged by your clever kid…within reason. Enjoy the verbal play and witty rejoinders. Be the adult. Let them win occasionally. You are building your relationship, day by day. Let them see you as an intelligent partner.

5. They may be thinking way beyond their chronological age. And, you may treat them intellectually, in many instances, like they are young adults. But keep an awareness of their real age and provide age-appropriate experiences, too. Kids need to play and fool around…no matter how smart they are.

6. You are the parent. Set firm guidelines if you are being overwhelmed by your child and challenged about everything. You may want to discuss things with your child and let them make many, many choices, but consider having several stock phrases to end the discussions when necessary:

   "I am the parent and that is my final decision."

   "I'll give you three minutes to present your point of view, and I will listen with an open mind, but then I will determine what we will do."

7. Help your child develop appropriate social skills. Your child often isn't as adorable to others as to you. When you see your child antagonizing people with his/her brainy behavior or verbal onslaught, take the time in private to practice alternative behaviors. Brainstorm different ways to share a point of view or a comment on issues. Help them be aware of how others think and feel.

8. Find a great mentor for your child besides you, an older friend or adult, or an organization where they can be stimulated, fit in and feel accepted. There are clubs and groups in many communities and on the Internet that revolve around interests like chess or cards or antique toy soldiers. While you monitor their involvement, allow them their passions.

Linda Levitt

6"THE KID ON OVERDRIVE"

THE VERY ACTIVE KID

Linda Levitt

"THE KID ON OVERDRIVE"
THE VERY ACTIVE KID

When my son was eight months old, he could open a dead bolt. He wasn't even walking yet. He was still getting around in one of those doughnut-shaped walkers with wheels. He'd wait until I I was in the shower and then he'd initiate his escape. He'd scoot it over to the heavy, oak front door where, on tiptoe, he'd reach up and unlock the dead bolt, pull open its six-foot width, unlatch the metal security screen, jockey into the opening between the two doors, bump down the double threshold, scoot across the brick patio, unlatch the child-proof gate and race across our cul-de-sac and out into the street, all with less time than it took me to soap up, twirl and rinse off.

I have this mental image of myself, wrapped in only a towel, wet hair streaming behind me, chasing my son down the middle of Oregon Avenue at 6:30 in the morning. I'm screaming. With his tiny face turned gleefully over his shoulder, he is laughing at me as he skates madly down the asphalt in his walker.

Linda Levitt

NOTES NOTES NOTES NOTES <u>NOTES</u>
on the Kid on Overdrive

CHARACTERISTICS OF

"THE KID ON OVERDRIVE"

I woke up for years to a little body sitting on my stomach, arms full of games shouting, "Hey, Mommy, get up! It's almost morning. How about a couple hands of Five Card Stud?"

- Always busy

- Keeps in motion with their body, brain, hands, mouth until they drop

- Fidgets, restless, moves legs, gets up often

- Needs to be moving in order to think

- Short attention span or unfocused until they fixate on something

- Trouble following directions

- Often misplaces things

- Tendency to seem bored— tunes out

- Rarely "lives up to potential"

- Has trouble going through "established channels"

- Is often a rule-breaker

- Likes the thrill of dangerous things

- Procrastinator, or no follow-through

- Impatient, low frustration level, low tolerance threshold

- Organizational issues

- Can be overly sensitive to noise, light, crowds, clothing

Linda Levitt

"THE KID ON OVERDRIVE"

When asked to stop singing and pounding at the dinner table, my child replied, "I'm not singing, I'm humming. I'm not pounding, I'm drumming!"

GOOD NEWS ABOUT THE VERY ACTIVE KID

- Their exuberance is contagious.

- You don't need an alarm clock.

- They are alert and avid learners.

- They take advantage of opportunities to try many things.

- They are the first ones to have fun on the playground, at the Science Museum, at the pet store.

- They are joyful to watch when playing outside and interacting with the environment.

- Their youthful energy often translates into a "go get 'em" attitude in later life.

- They are passionate about their interests and throw themselves in wholeheartedly.

- Their imagination is profoundly exciting.

- They are the creators and problem-solvers the world is looking for.

"THE KID ON OVERDRIVE"

When my son was a two-year old, he ran away in the busy
Safeway parking lot and I swatted his diapered bottom.
He froze in astonishment and began to scream at the top of his voice,
"Help! Help! Blood! Murder!"

BAD NEWS ABOUT THE VERY ACTIVE KID

- They break stuff.

- They keep you from sleep.

- They do things that are dangerous.

- They need lots of space.

- Unfinished "junk" is everywhere.

- They are difficult to keep track of; taking them anywhere is a problem.

- They interrupt others or butt in line, not seeming to understand taking turns. (Doesn't enhance popularity.)

- Trouble with rules in general 'cuz rules don't apply to them.

- They make other people (especially teachers) nervous.

- They drive older people crazy.

- They may have difficulty making friends.

- They may have trouble getting along on organized teams with rules.

- "I'm bored," is an often heard refrain.

Linda Levitt

WHAT YOU CAN DO TO SUPPORT "THE KID ON OVERDRIVE"

1. Explain the rules and describe appropriate behavior you expect from your child BEFORE you go places. Practice it at home.

2. Don't take your child to places where they WILL embarrass you or bother other people, until they can perform acceptably. Your child does not want to create conflict. Why force it?

3. Remove objects that you don't want your child to touch before they break them. Give them lots of other old, interesting stuff to examine and take apart.

4. Make the time to help them practice the use of and handling of fragile or sort-of dangerous things with your supervision. Help them learn to be proud of being careful and trustworthy.

5. Spend lots of time outdoors. Children who spend most of their time outside are calmer, happier children.

6. Find a school where there is a large play area and where recess is considered an important part of the curriculum.

7. If your child can walk to school or ride their bike (with or without you), try to do that. If not, make certain they get to school in time to play outside before the school day begins.

8. Talk to the teacher about alternate ways to work in the classroom. Are there centers to move about? Can they stand at the back counter to work? Can you provide lap desks and floor mats for kids who work better on the floor? Can frequent breaks be encouraged?

9. Limit TV, videos, computers. Don't allow them to be used as baby-sitters for your child. Work together to pick out a few acceptable shows and games. Intersperse them with hands-on, active play.

10. Make certain your child gets plenty of sleep. Whether they seem tired or not, very active kids need as much rest as other children.

11. Read about nutrition and feed your child well. Healthy food is brain and body fuel. You are what you eat.

12. Keep your child busy with appropriate activities. Take advantage of the many places and programs for children that your community provides. There are walks and hikes and bird-watching, library programs, environmental agencies, animal rescue facilities, art programs, creative dance and music programs. Many programs today are sponsored by non-profit agencies or educational institutions and are free of cost. Fight "boredom" by filling their minds with great thoughts and experiences. Research shows that the most successful young adults were exposed to and had the opportunities to explore many things and places as children.

13. Teach them to work. Helping around the house, in the yard and in your community burns lots of energy. Teach your child at a young age to expend their energy on accomplishing good works. A freshly waxed dresser or a swept sidewalk is something to be proud of and will help your child develop a work ethic for their future.

14. Praise your child often for behaviors you want to keep. Help them learn self-talk to monitor themselves by analyzing what they are doing and what they could do differently.

15. Make time for imaginative play, body-calming exercise, relaxing, and self-fulfilling mind games.

16. Consider enrolling them in martial arts.

Linda Levitt

6 "THE HUMAN SEARCH ENGINE" 9

KID WITH A MILLION INTERESTS

"THE HUMAN SEARCH ENGINE"
KID WITH A MILLION INTERESTS

My son didn't pick dinosaurs, or dogs, or cars for his first passionate, out-of-sync interest. He picked "Implements of Destruction". It started with paper towel rolls, Lego-size swords and harmless, kiddie construction equipment, like three-inch bulldozers. But it quickly escalated to bigger and sharper things. He became fascinated with weapons. At age three we went often to the public library where he repeatedly checked out all the books on guns, weapons, war and bombs. His favorite was an enormous, in full-color, highly detailed, coffee table sized picture edition of Military Attire and War Paraphernalia.

He'd lie on the floor and pour over each page memorizing the dress uniform, battle regalia and implements of destruction of every armed force in the known world. One Christmas we unfortunately gave him a video game inappropriately named Medal of Honor, and were forced to destroy it after he stood in front of the screen without moving for the whole week, mesmerized by the weapon cache and visual attack arsenal.

Years later, I met a mother from our former preschool who said she had ALWAYS wanted to meet me. I expected a compliment about my school garden. No. She told me that while driving our, then four-year old, sons on a field trip, they had played the game "CATEGORIES" in the car. She recalled that instead of "Food" or "Animals" my son had chosen "Weapons."

"I was terrified," she sweetly informed me. "I never knew a child who could recite the names of so many guns and knives and incendiary devices! I expected his parents to be some crazed survivalists... or in jail!"

Linda Levitt

www.notesonthehumansearchengine.goget'em

CHARACTERISTICS OF

"THE HUMAN SEARCH ENGINE"

"Who? What? When? Where? Why? Why? Why?"

• Very curious: look closely, touch everything, sniff, smell, taste and ask "why" long into the night.

• Talk and interrupt with no inhibitions anytime/anyplace with their questions.

• Ask more questions about your answers and correct you or argue with you if they disagree. Then, ask another adult the same question, just to check on you.

• Ask "BIG" questions like- "If God loves us, why is there war and killing over religion?"

• Process your answers carefully then ask you deeper questions about what you said (putting you on notice not to make anything up to get rid of them).

• Examine/take apart valuable and live objects.

• Explore multiple interests at the same time! May develop deep passions about subjects and want to know EVERYTHING.

• May change passions quickly, when they've learned what they wanted to know.

• Demand the opportunity to do dangerous things…just to see for themselves if the "danger" applies to them…like speed, gravity and fire.

• Their interests may be WAY out-of -sync with their age.

　　　　Linda Levitt

"THE HUMAN SEARCH ENGINE"

When walking through a museum chocked full of WWII memorabilia and aircraft, the eight–year-old sighed and said, "This is MY Woodstock."

GOOD NEWS ABOUT THE KID WITH A MILLION INTERESTS

- Curious kids are great learners.

- Curious people invent new things, question the WAY things are, and often change and improve the world.

- They are unafraid to try new things.

- Exploration in-depth often leads to new things to explore, thus creating a cycle of never-ending learning.

- Their passion for topics is invigorating and contagious.

- Their minds seem to store everything.

- They keep adults alert and stimulated.

- They are often a great asset to a classroom by initiating discussions and opening up other topics of interest.

- They often become great readers, explorers and creators, sometimes all at once!

- They love to go interesting places, just to look around.

- Scientists, inventors, artists, philosophers HAD to be curious kids.

"THE HUMAN SEARCH ENGINE"

As I was frantically driving him across town to yet another important enrichment activity, my son leaned across the car seat, touched my arm gently and said, "Mom, I know you're doing this for my own good and I'll appreciate it when I'm older, but right now, I'm trying hard not to hate you!"

BAD NEWS ABOUT THE KID WITH A MILLION INTERESTS

- Endless questioning can drive parents and teachers crazy.

- After a while, the tendency is to try to make them STOP, instead of encouraging their interests.

- Questions interrupt movies, lectures, class.

- Some of the questions are painful, embarrassing or just plain hysterical.

- Adults have to work hard just to keep up.

- Curious kids break stuff.

- They are often interested in many things and they make HUGE messes with their experiments and collections.

- The variety and voracity is expensive.

- They seem to be ALWAYS right, so be prepared to back up your facts.

- These kids may need supervision long into their teenage years because they often are curious about things that are illegal or dangerous.

- Out-of-sync learning is educationally and socially difficult. School will need supplementing/ your child may not relate well to his/her peer group.

Linda Levitt

WHAT YOU CAN DO TO SUPPORT "THE HUMAN SEARCH ENGINE"

1. Really listen to their questions. Try to avoid asking them to leave you alone and be quiet. Those kind of slights will wound the avid learner. As the valuable adult in their lives, you want to encourage intellectual expenditures of thought.

2. If you can't stand their questions for one more second, have a loving grandparent or friend on your speed-dial and have your child call them.

3. Answer current questions as politely as you can, or say "I don't know that YET." And, then help them find out. As soon as they are able, teach them to find answers on their own by experimentation, researching on the Internet, consulting reference books, knowledgeable people, hours of reading. Fill their lives and their futures with potential resources for learning.

4. Have a notebook where you jot down each important question, one on each page, or have them write the questions if they are old enough. Refer back to this frequently so you can remember what they have asked you about. See if you can find new information in the news, library, in magazines or about events of interest to share with them. They might have already forgotten what they asked you about, but you are validating their thoughts and teaching them that learning takes effort.

5. Use your time in the car wisely. Talk to them as you drive places. Take away the hand-held games, turn off the radio, close the cartoon book and involve yourselves in question and discussion sessions. Keep texts in the back seat that are easy to reference, like "Did You Know That....," fact books, atlases or Brain Quest.

6. Set aside some time each day to really explore in-depth an area where your child has a multitude of questions. For example, become "Shark People" for a week and get library books, buy puzzles, rent movies, visit an aquarium or search a live Internet site. Share their interest, become a researcher and a fan with them.

7. Fill their lives with hands-on activities: water, sand, mud, paper, used appliances, junk, recycled stuff, fabric, art supplies, magnets, metal, building and climbing apparatus...tools. Let them explore and draw their own conclusions, formulate new questions and explore again.

8. Fill your home with reference material. Post maps at eye level on your walls. Have a globe, atlas, compass, protractor, and a calculator sitting right on their desks. Keep fact books like dictionaries, thesauruses, atlases, almanacs, travel magazines, science magazines, BIG Books of World Records, bus schedules, etc. where they are easy to flip through and browse. Smart kids like facts.

9. Take your child everywhere you can. Hikes, trips, movies, museums, art shows, concerts, animal rescue events, restaurants, nature trails, community meetings. Open their minds. Expand their world.

10. Everybody needs one good friend who they can relate to. If your child is out-of-sync with their peer group, find an older child, a member of your church or community, or an organization of the web that shares the same interests as your child. Be it chess, model trains or baseball cards, it is a joy to share your passions and be able to fit in.

Linda Levitt

"THE FUNNY, FUNKY KID"

THE AMUSING, UNINHIBITED NONCONFORMIST

"THE FUNNY, FUNKY KID"
THE AMUSING. UNINHIBITED NONCONFORMIST

By the time my sister's daughter, Sara, was in late elementary school, their family had come to an agreement. It was understood that you asked DAD for answers to your questions about math and science and MOM about grammar and Spanish. It was a joke in their house, among the mathematically brilliant husband and daughters, that Mom hated story problems and they all liked to torment her with them.

One night when tucking her almost-teenage daughter into bed, the two of them got on the important topic of the "Birds and the Bees." It was the appropriate parental time to discuss these things. After the conversation, Mom felt she had done a pretty good job explaining love and life and sex to her beautiful daughter.

She asked if there were any questions, letting her daughter know that she was willing to talk to her about anything.

"Well, I just have one, Mom," Sara replied, sweetly.

"Yes?" Mom asked, gently encouraging her.

"Well, Mom," she replied with a very serious expression on her face, "If a train is going east at fifty miles an hour and it passes another train going west at 60 miles an hour..."

Linda Levitt

Notes on the Funny Funky Kid

Notes on the Funny Funky Kid

Notes on the Funny Funky Kid

Notes on the Funny Funky Kid

CHARACTERISTICS OF
"THE FUNNY, FUNKY KID"

When I found a scorpion in my underwear drawer one scary morning, my five-year-old just laughed and said, "Mom, I think he was on a panty raid."

- Understands humor at a very young age.

- Loves jokes, puns, riddles, plays on words.

- Finds cartoons hilarious.

- Enjoys all forms of verbal and written humor; TV, movies, theater, puppet shows, joke books, comics, satire.

- Often has a droll point of view on events and situations.

- Interjects their "humor" into conversations.

- Will tease or "razz" others mercilessly.

- Memorizes or makes up jokes or funny stories and tells them over and over.

- Pours over the adult comics and editorial cartoons in the newspaper, asking insightful questions.

- Dresses with total disregard for fashion.

- Dresses as though they've never looked in a mirror.

- Often wears "costumes" or bizarre clothing.

- Doesn't seem to mind being different.

- Is attracted to weird others.

Linda Levitt

"THE FUNNY, FUNKY KID"

"Happy birthday, Mommy! How old are you today? YOU'RE FIFTY? Oh, I'm sorry!"

GOOD NEWS ABOUT THE AMUSING, UNINHIBITED, NONCONFORMIST

- They ARE funny!

- They often have clever additions to conversations.

- They add levity to life.

- Laughter is healthy and contagious.

- Being the "funny guy" can help a child makes friends.

- Funny kids are fun to be around.

- Their humor often disguises the real issues but can be used as a springboard for discussions on issues that really matter.

- Their choice of attire is hilarious. Who doesn't want to be a pirate or a princess?

- They tend to choose associates and interests that are fascinating.

- The creative spirit of an artist-in-the making is powerful.

- They stand out in this crowded world.

"THE FUNNY, FUNKY KID"

"When I grow up and be a rock star, Mommy, will you still love me and clap when I sing those dirty words?"

BAD NEWS ABOUT THE AMUSING, UNINHIBITED, NONCONFORMIST

- Some kids use being funny to draw attention to themselves.

- They can disrupt classes, public events, AND important conversations.

- Their humor can be wicked or hurtful.

- They often enjoy ribald or inappropriate humor and will repeat it where it is definitely NOT funny.

- They tell the same jokes and stories over and over again and laugh at themselves.

- Their use of humor or language can be out-of-sync with age and offend people.

- Verbal teasing can get out of hand.

- Humor often is used to disguise or divert from real issues, problems, or work needing to be done.

- Bizarre forms of dress and costumes seem less funny on a twelve-year old than a five year old.

- Their lack of a "social filter" or weirdness can make it difficult to fit in and limit places they are welcomed and accepted.

Linda Levitt

WHAT YOU CAN DO TO SUPPORT "THE FUNNY, FUNKY KID"

1. Laugh, and laugh some more. Let them tell their jokes a million times and share with them in what they find funny. You are your child's first and most important audience.

2. Encourage appropriate use of wit by talking with your child about the cartoons or comics or sitcoms. Discuss the jokes and what they see as funny and decide with them whether it really IS funny.

3. Use the points they see as non-conforming or humorous to clarify the real situations on which the humor is based. Often times "jokes" are recycled facts from the past that weren't or aren't really funny. Use these situations to talk about history, prejudices, social change.

4. Develop your child's sense of moral character by discussing the deeper topics that humor often times covers up: fear, bullying, loneliness, prejudice. Help use humor to educate your child into the "big issues" of life.

5. Humor defuses anger and conflict. You can help your child use their sense of humor to see different takes on events in their lives and help them deal with them.

6. Humor and laughter, optimism and resiliency help build and repair the immune system, reduce stress and increase life expectancy. Recognizing and enjoying the brighter side of life will help you both in times of distress.

7. Try to work with your child to uncover the reality behind their banter. If humor is used as a disguise or a cover-up, some painful issues are best

recognized, addressed and discussed even if a humorous twist is the best survival technique in the end.

8. Recognize that funny people are fun to be around. Laughter is a great tool in making friends. Witty and happy people are often popular and the life of the party.

9. Allow your child to dress themselves and express themselves in reasonable ways. Their imagination is expressed in their clothing and costume selection. Who is it really going to hurt?

10. If you must have some guidelines for their attire, work with your child to choose them. If they must dress in certain ways to associate in "your circle," make sure you allow them the opportunity to dress their way in "their circle."

11. If your child chooses unusual pastimes, attire, friends and associates, keep the lines of communication open. Monitoring your children's activities is your JOB as a parent! But… controlling them is not the only option.

12. Introduce your child to people more interesting than yourself.

13. Keep a large collection of boots.

14. Lighten up!

Linda Levitt

THE PERFECTIONIST

"I HAVE TO BE RIGHT! IT HAS TO BE RIGHT!"

THE PERFECTIONIST
"I HAVE TO BE RIGHT! IT HAS TO BE RIGHT!"

After drawing intently for several hours on a huge piece of art paper, my seven-year old son had created an intricate castle, complete with moat, parapets and turrets.

He turned his paper to the left and right, carefully examining his finished product. Then, he methodically penciled in hundreds of perfectly round, tiny black circles along the outer walls, which he explained to his mother and brother, were monkeys.

The next day the picture came out again, in order to "make it perfect."

Briskly he sharpened his pencil and began to painstakingly attach VERY small "S" shapes to the bottom of each circle.

We watched him draw for a quite awhile, then asked him what in the world he was doing?

"I'm adding their tails," he replied solemnly.

And, for a very long time, he did.

Linda Levitt

Notes on
The Perfectionist

- ■ _____
- ■ _____
- ■ _____
- ■ _____
- ■ _____
- ■ _____
- ■ _____
- ■ _____
- ■ _____
- ■ _____
- ■ _____

CHARACTERISTICS OF

THE PERFECTIONIST

"I HAVE TO BE RIGHT! IT HAS TO BE RIGHT!"

My seventeen year old son commented proudly last week, "When I get finished with football season I think I'll take up some hobbies, like...well, like flexibility."

- Driven by routines, maintaining order, and control

- Highly competitive

- Expects too much of themselves

- Expects too much of others

- Fears failure

- May have low self-confidence

- Comes unglued with things that don't go their way

- May underachieve if they feel they can't be perfect

- Often seems stressed or sad or unsatisfied

- Avoids trying new things

- Procrastinates

- May appear very unhappy in school, cry, complain

- Often self-critical

- Avoids school assignments, produces incomplete work

- May choose to work very slowly and meticulously on assignments

- Often seems to overreact to criticism

Linda Levitt

"IT HAS TO BE RIGHT! I HAVE TO BE RIGHT!"

As I'm dropping my son off at SuperKid Chess Lessons, he turns to me and says "Maybe YOU should come in with me, Mom, instead of waiting in the car. You might learn something!"

GOOD NEWS ABOUT THE PERFECTIONIST

- Expectations to do well MAY lead to high achievement.

- Excellence is attainable and a good sense of accomplishment can occur when the "perfect" part is left out.

- "Quality" is a reasonable life plan.

- Some leaders are perfectionists and do more than their share of the work leaving the rest of us free to fool around.

- Their houses are usually pretty clean.

"IT HAS TO BE RIGHT! I HAVE TO BE RIGHT!"

Every morning his bedroom floor is littered with discarded shirts, shorts and socks he has rejected in tears because they "itch."

BAD NEWS ABOUT THE PERFECTIONIST

- Perfectionism goes beyond excellence AND provides little satisfaction. The results never seem to be good enough. Perfectionism isn't about doing your best; it's about accepting yourself only if you are perfect.

- Perfectionists want order and routines which often disrupt other people's lives and mental health.

- Perfectionists need control and want to control others.

- To feel good about themselves, perfectionists often put other people down.

- Perfectionists give unsolicited advice that is irritating to others but reassures perfectionists of how smart they are.

- Perfectionists often procrastinate to delay making a wrong decision.

- They often run late because they do too much.

- Perfectionists are not happy with second place.

- Mistakes make them fearful, limiting what new things they are willing to try.

- When someone tries to mess with their plans or their routines, perfectionists get angry at the person who tries to change their orderly life, fearing that things will end up in a mess.

Linda Levitt

- To balance the perfectionist in the family, there always seems to be a "bad kid" or an under-achiever or a family pattern where a spouse is made to feel inadequate or less intelligent by the perfectionistic one.

- Perfectionists can experience great trouble in school; sadness, anger, crying, avoidance, incomplete work, slow production of meticulously completed assignments.

- Perfectionists are often highly self-critical, have low self-confidence and overreact to criticism from teachers, parents, peers.

STRATEGIES TO SUPPORT
THE PERFECTIONIST

1. Set expectations that are reasonable for your kids. Home environments influence and perpetuate perfectionism. Children can learn perfectionism from their parent/parents. If someone in your family takes on too much or avoids including your children in projects around the home, you are giving your children the message that they are not capable of doing things well enough. If things must be "your way," "the right way," your children may believe they have to be like you to be loved. Teach your child by monitoring your own perfectionistic behavior.

2. Look carefully at what is happening in your family. A chaotic home environment- divorce, split homes, constant conflict, abuse, and stress can contribute to perfectionist thinking. Children may conclude that they are part of the problem because they can't make things better. A troubled family increases feelings of failure and not being enough.

3. Practice flexibility in your home and schedule. Kids need routines, not rigidity. If you model only structured and organized days, your child will have difficulty adjusting to change.

4. Model for and explain to your children that there is more than one correct way to do almost everything in life, and try to convince yourself.

5. Create an environment of acceptance in your home. Let your children know they are loved for who they are, not for what they do. This will help them have the courage to try new things.

Linda Levitt

6. Tell your children that aiming for excellence and aiming for perfection are two different goals. "Success" is what results from hard work and effort.

7. Help kids to learn to feel good when they've DONE their very best, not BEEN the very best. Your comments can set the stage. "You worked very hard," "You spent lots of time on that," can help them learn to evaluate themselves in a healthy way and encourage self-talk like, "I learned a lot," "I challenged myself."

8. Many of the most successful people in our world experienced multiple catastrophic failures in their lives. Talk about some of these people with your children, read their biographies, go to motivational lectures and meet with people who are willing to share their failures with an audience. Make your child aware of the feelings that people have when they fail and help them learn how to turn these emotions to their advantage.

9. Don't let your child believe you are perfect. Be open to sharing your own mistakes and what you learned from them. Letting your child see you laugh at your own mistakes can help them laugh at theirs.

10. Teach your child that we all learn more and best from our mistakes. Share some of your biggest "bloopers." Don't be so self-critical. If you must point out your mistakes, then congratulate yourself on a good job in front of your child.

11. Work with your child to practice ways to deal with criticism. They will be criticized all their lives by teachers and coaches and friends. The right words and body language to accept criticism from others will help your child have the opportunity to learn from it.

13. Bright children are often very critical of others. Help them learn how to be constructive in their criticism. Talk about and model "small talk" and positive comments and compliments, and what positive relationships can do for themselves and for others.

14. If your child is often bragging, talk with them about how this makes others feel. Help them learn to congratulate themselves privately and help them learn how to compliment and congratulate others graciously.

15. Teach them to breathe, balance, meditate, relax, and forgive.

Linda Levitt

Linda's Labels

Linda Levitt

LINDA'S LABELS AND DEFINITIONS

GIFTED

The United States federal government's definition of GIFTED and TALENTED students is as follows:

The term "gifted and talented" when used in respect to students, children, or youth means students, children, or youth who give evidence of high performance capability in areas such as intellectual, creative, artistic, or leadership capacity, or in specific academic fields, and who require services or activities not ordinarily provided by the school in order to fully develop such capabilities. (P.L. 103–382, Title XIV, p. 388)

ATTENTION DEFICIT DISORDER (ADD)

The American Heritage Dictionary's definition of ATTENTION DEFICIT DISORDER:

NOUN: abbr. ADD A syndrome, usually diagnosed in childhood, characterized by a persistent pattern of impulsiveness, a short attention span, and often hyperactivity, and interfering especially with academic, occupational, and social performance.

ATTENTION DEFICIT HYPERACTIVE DISORDER (ADHD)

Wikipedia, the free encyclopedia, defines ADHD:

Attention deficit hyperactivity disorder (ADHD) is considered to be a neurological syndrome that exhibits symptoms such as hyperactivity, forgetfulness, mood shifts, poor impulse control, and distractibility, when judged to be chronic, as symptoms of a neurological pathology. It is seen in both children and adults and is believed to affect between 3% to 5% of the human population.

Linda Levitt

INDIGO CHILDREN

On the World Wide Web, ROANOKE.COM says this about INDIGO CHILDREN:

The definition of an Indigo child varies depending on which New Age Web site you visit, but most believers who have these children seem to agree that they have shared characteristics: They're smarter and more emotionally aware than their parents; they're frequently defiant of authority; and sometimes they're very intuitive and possibly psychic.

COMPLETELY SPOILED BRAT- "CSB"

The collective wisdom of the famous authors and mothers of the current fast-selling collection, LifeLines, defines CSB as:

The child who has been so indulged by well-meaning parents that he/she grows up believing that his/her every want is a need, every whim is a must-have, every antic worth recording... resulting in a child nobody enjoys being around.

TERRIFIC KID

Your kid.

SURVIVAL STRATEGIES FOR WORKING SUCCESSFULLY WITH SCHOOLS

Linda Levitt

SURVIVAL STRATEGIES FOR WORKING SUCCESSFULLY WITH SCHOOLS

When our children go off to school, we are releasing our most precious possessions to a large institutionalized puzzle where they are just one small piece, instead of the only piece. Our children will now spend most of the day… and all the rest of their childhood in school. When choosing a school, we send our children to places and people we want to trust and whom we believe will do the very best for our child. The schools you choose need to work.

It does not always happen that way…easily. Gifted kids, our terrific kids, often require multiple juggling acts, conferences and interventions to make their placement in schools successful. Working with teachers and administrations is a talent and an art you'll want to learn if your want the best for your child.

Gifted, terrific kids are not always the easiest kids in the class.

Potentially…

- The gifted kid is the teacher's pet and becomes the class pariah.

- The gifted kid is always done with their work quickly so they become the errand boy…instead of the aerospace engineer you had in mind since they spend all their educational hours helping the teacher.

- The gifted kid becomes a tutor for other kids, helping them with their work instead of receiving accelerated, appropriate instruction.

- The gifted kid, the terrific kid, gets more busy work when they finish or double the work if they receive pullout services…and thus refuse to work.

- The gifted kid knows all the answers and is constantly interrupting or challenging the teacher. They thus become "a problem in class."

- The gifted, terrific kid already knows all the answers or did all the work last year, or isn't the LEAST BIT INTERESTED in what the teacher is trying to teach, so instead of learning anything, school becomes a place to daydream, play mind games, disrupt.

Linda Levitt

If you want your child to receive the best education they possible can AND fit in and be happy, you need some strategies to approach your school successfully.

Strategies

1. Spend some time on the campus and in the classrooms of the school where you want your child to attend. Don't just rely on someone else's evaluation or a public report on the qualities of the school. List the things you really want for your child in a school and check to see if there is a fair match. I sent my two sons off to their first school because of the size of the playground, the amount of trees on the campus and the fact that they let kids climb them! We all have different priorities and perspectives about what schools are about.

2. Look at the high ratios of kids to staff in schools. No staff is as familiar with your child as you are. Nor are they as interested in your child as you are. Schedule an introductory conference. Take the time to listen to the staff about their observations, concerns and suggestions about your child. Take notes. Ask questions. Observe on campus and in the classroom if you are allowed to. While you are there, respect their space as you would in anyone's business. But, see if the purported programs actually are in action and how they work.

3. Create a spirit of cooperation and teamwork between school and home. Before there are problems, get involved. Your child needs to see collaboration, not criticism and competition. They do not need to view home and school as two completely unconnected places. For your child to feel secure enough to be successful in school, you need to set the stage. Make all your initial contacts with the school positive. Go to meetings and fundraisers. Attend Open House. Find out what the expectations are for the courses. Attend class events. Send in things requested from the teacher. Follow school rules and get your child there on time. If you haven't spent a

day in a public school lately, *do so before you complain.* It will be an eye-opener. Put yourself in the place of the staff who, most likely, are trying to do their very best under pretty trying circumstances!

4. Don't let your own school experiences color and affect how you view your children's current experiences. They simply are not the same and you can't let them control what you *do* today for your own kids. If there are problems at school, the school is not totally to blame. Keep the team concept in mind and accept your responsibility as parents and the part your child plays. If you want to make school and school communication successful, instead of looking for someone/something to blame, work on creating interventions and solutions.

5. Think of schools as a big business with lots of competition. Think of your child as a client. There are workable solutions for every problem. Approach your school as a business that needs to be effective by creating successful products and customers. Keep yourself up-to-date on what is new in education as it pertains to the needs and concerns of your child. There are amazing sites on the internet that address school issues. You can be an effective parent for your child if you work WITH the school creating a mutually respectful and supportive relationship.

**Note that the above advice comes from a parent who just spent the last two weeks in an enormous fight with my high school senior's school to get his grade in Economics upgraded so that he could play in the final championship football games. I was awesome. They were wrong. I was articulate. We were all at fault. I was correct in my advocacy and anger. BUT, we got into that exhausting mess because I ignored my own above stated good advice.

Linda Levitt

ADVOCATING
FOR YOUR CHILD

ADVOCATING FOR YOUR CHILD

YOU ARE THEIR GREATEST SUPPORTER
AND THEIR FIRST LINE OF DEFENSE

Advocacy is active support.

As your child's parent, you are their primary support system. You are their first teacher and for many years, you have the most influence on your child. You play a key role in determining where their life will lead. You must advocate for your child's success in school.

Terrific children that are not experiencing success in their classrooms are in need of help. The earlier they get support and appropriate intervention, the better for them! Parental interest and involvement is first step. Parents must make the effort. Teachers and friends can certainly help.

From the educators' perspective, some parents do seem to act too aggressively in demanding what they believe is the best for their children. Parents, read about parent advocacy. Easy to access sites are on the internet. Follow good advice. It takes cooperation from the people involved in your child's education to make changes. Make them your friends. Work with them.

From the educators' perspective, some parents are not aggressive enough. They seem to leave everything to the school, expect the teachers to do it all until there is a disaster. Parents, read about strategies for success-ful parent advocacy. Follow good advice. You cannot expect the schools to know it all and to do everything right for every child. Surprisingly, teachers and administrators may not be smarter or more knowledgeable about your kid and what may be best for them than you are. Lots of teachers are stuck in a

Linda Levitt

classroom all day! That can really limit their exposure to new ideas. If your school placement is not working for your child, advocate. Read. Research. Find a support group in your community or on the internet and ask for their advice or direction.

Advocacy's Key Points:

1. No school is any better than the person/people standing in front of your child for those six important hours each day. That person or those people who are standing there need to be interacting with your child in ways that will maximize your child's success. Nobody ever forgets horrible school experiences. They stay with us for our lifetime. They shape our lives. Gifted, terrific children are at-risk of "being left behind." Nothing can replace an appropriate education for a good start in life. Encouragement and guidance by quality, well-meaning teachers is invaluable. Time wasted in less-than-dynamic education can not be gotten back. Your child's self-esteem is paramount to their success in life. It is worth any amount of effort you must expend to find an appropriate education for your child.

2. You know a whole lot more about your child and their background and their interests than the school knows. Don't be afraid to represent your child's needs and ask for accommodations to help them reach their potential.

   Make certain you know about the laws in your state and district and school policy as it relates to your child. Keep informed on gifted education and gifted strategies and other programs that might impact your child's education. As a voracious supporter of your child, you may have explored more and read more and seen more than many of the educators you are working with. And, you may know more. Policy and interventions with gifted and terrific children are changing. Be open to sharing your ideas and encouraging change gracefully. Listen to the responses of the staff working with your child. Negotiate. Seek advice from other professionals or parents if your views don't mesh. But, don't let yourself think it is someone else's job to seek appropriate education for your child.

3. Don't give up. The brighter the child, the more they might need alternate strategies and placement. If you don't like, or disagree with, the answers you are getting from your first source, keep looking. There are lots of new things being tried to enhance the education of our brightest learners. And, there are a multitude of school choices available for children these days. Depending on where you live, what your family needs consist of, what options are available to you to choose from and your long-range goals for your child, you have choices to consider.

Public schools in your neighborhood might be the very best choice and may be willing to adjust the teachers, the classrooms, the requirements or the services for your child. If not, the gamut of private schools and charter schools and online schools and home schools and night schools needs to be explored. Universities have programs, parent groups and art schools have programs. Each child's needs are different, and as your child ages, their needs will change. Think flexibility and persistence.

Underachieving, Unmotivated, At-Risk Learner

Linda Levitt

Underachieving, Unmotivated, At-Risk Learner

Strategies to Help the Bright Underachiever
Be More Successful in School

The information in this section is in my mind, daily, since I have two bright children, one still struggling through high school and one approaching middle school, attempting to actively underachieve. My children have fallen into this deep pit of underachievement, primarily due to parental errors and I continually strive to find ways to help them locate the quickest way out.

Many bright children become miserable underachievers. It is a lifelong problem. Some seem bored and lazy. Some just don't get the work done. Some procrastinate until it's too late. Some won't do ANYTHING if they can't be the best…or do it perfectly. Some kids do not want to be "the best" at anything that involves doing it in the classroom. Some of our children are under challenged, some are unmotivated. Many become just plain unsuccessful.

Often bright children flounder in educational situations until they fall apart, (or their families fall apart) or they fail or just mentally give up. You don't have to quote statistics or read research to know that a huge percentage of gifted people never reach their potential. Just look at yourself, around the Thanksgiving dinner table, or into your own family history.

Popular opinion may be that gifted children can make it and find their way all on their own. This just isn't the case, especially at school. Although gifted children do possess exceptional skills, intelligence and talents, many will not be able to make it without our encouragement, guidance and support in getting on the right track in life and staying there.

Linda Levitt

Kids manage to perform unsuccessfully or far below their ability in school for many reasons. Here are only some of them:

• There may be problems or conflict in parenting at home that are stressful or confusing to the child.

• The child may lack confidence in their own abilities and fear failure.

• Learning may have started out so "easy" in the younger grades that when school got tougher they lacked the organizational ability, the discipline to extend the effort and/or the study skills necessary for success.

• Early learning may have started out so easy that they rushed through tasks or put off needed work and procrastinated so often that this style becomes their style of approaching school.

• Because they are so bright, they may have been skipped over material and missed sub skills of higher learning and may lack basic skills necessary for higher success.

• Over time, boredom in school may have led to them to "tune out" what goes on in the classroom.

• Class work may be so below their intellectual level of interest that they lose interest in school early-on and simply refuse to do assignments that seem meaningless.

• They may be mentally under challenged in class but overwhelmed with tedious unnecessary "busy work."

• There may be underlying learning/behavior disorders - low reading comprehension, dysgraphia, auditory processing disorders, visual tracking immaturity, sleep issues, or depression (the twice-exceptional child) that inhibit success.

• There may be learned homework and long-range project issues: disorganization, irresponsibility, procrastination.

• There may be test-taking issues: anxiety, peer competition, carelessness, poor writing/spelling.

• Social issues and interactions may be interfering with learning.

• They may have "learned helplessness" from parents and teachers who have done too much for them.

• Overindulgent parents may have taught the child that they don't have to work to get what they want in life.

• Under-indulgent parents may have left the child with too much else to do to put school as a top priority.

• Because they are bright, children may have been given too much power, too many choices and too much freedom too soon, treated like they are young adults too early. This can result in the resentment of reasonable control and responsibility that goes with school.

• Child-rearing strategies may have taught the child that his efforts won't change the outcomes.

• Child-rearing strategies may have taught the child that his best just isn't good enough.

It is scary and overwhelming to read over the potential causes for underachievement.

Linda Levitt

Interested teachers, family therapists or individual counselors can look at the above scenarios and sift through the child's life and provide some insight as to why a child is unsuccessful. Any of these might be worth exploring!

But the WHY of underachievement is less easy to change than the HOW to make tomorrow better. The easier fix is to work on teaching simple behaviors that will alter underachievement in your child. That means expectations, attitudes and responsibilities.

Underachievement Scenarios

Report Card Day
Social Studies class – Your child has not done well.
Potential comments from your <u>child</u>:

1. "That teacher is so mean. She hates me! She gave me a failing grade in Social Studies."

2. "I hate school. I sat in that stupid, boring class all quarter and I still failed Social Studies."

3. "I don't know what happened in Social Studies. I got another 'F'."

Report Card Day
Social Studies class – Your child has not done well.
Potential comments from <u>you</u>:

1. "That teacher is an idiot. She didn't teach you anything. Only losers go into education. I am going to let her have it!"

2. "That is your third 'F'. Why don't you do something?"

3. "How can you be so smart and be so dumb? You are grounded AND I'm taking away your computer AND your XBox!"

Believe me, these scenarios happen in many once-happy homes at the end of every grading period. Bright kids often fail. They just don't seem to get the cause and effect about school and studying and achievement or are unwilling to change their behavior to head for success.

Achievement Scenarios

Report Card Day-
Social Studies – Your child has not done well.
Potential comments from your <u>child</u>:

1. "That teacher is so mean. I don't like her! And, I got a failing grade in Social Studies"

2. "I hate school. But if I have to sit in that stupid, boring class all quarter I don't want to fail Social Studies. I need help".

3. "I don't know what happened. I got another "F". Can you meet with me and my teacher and get a plan so my grade will improve?"

Report Card Day
Social Studies class – Your child has not done well.
Potential comments from <u>parent</u>:

1. "We need to meet with you and your teacher ASAP! You seem to not be learning what you need to learn in that class. Let's make an appointment."

2. "That is your third "F". What's going on here? It's time to sit down with the school to do something for you that will help you out."

3. You must feel badly. You are so smart but it isn't showing up in your grades. We need to be something at home to help you change your studying style.

Wouldn't these conversations seem to be more likely to lead to success at the end of every grading period? Bright kids don't need to fail. They need to get the cause and effect about school and studying and achievement and be willing to change their behavior to head for success.

WHAT YOU CAN DO TO SUPPORT YOUR UNDERACHIEVER

FIRST, let's define underachievement as a discrepancy between ability and performance. Face it, we all underachieve in many areas. We only use like, 10% of our brain! All of us could do better in all aspects of our lives if we extended more effort, interest and time. What we are addressing here is kids who are not making it in school.

Common sense parenting, and reading PILES of articles and research has led me to the conclusion that underachievement can be modified and changed. Or, at least by a home-school connection, your child's level of achievement can be raised to the level of passing classes and heading toward a future…instead of them living under a bridge…or with you…forever.

Certain types of children ARE disorganized. Certain types of children ARE unmotivated. Certain types of children REFUSE to do homework…or do it and don't turn it in. Some kids are lazy. Kids have different mental and emotional issues, mature at different rates. Kids have varying levels of desire and motivation to achieve. But with a team approach involving parents/student/school, especially when starting at as early an age as possible, bright and talented children can learn to perform in schools in ways that minimize underachievement and that help their "terrificness" become more apparent.

To begin, each reader of this text has to define what they believe is meant by "underachievement." If you expect straight "A's" in advance placement classes from your child, then anything less than that is "underachieving." If you just want work to be turned in and tests passed so that your child doesn't fail, that is another. If you want the school to stop calling you, or your child is unhappy, dissatisfied and refuses to participate in areas where they have talents, then that is even another level of underachievement.

Families, including the child, need to determine and agree on what level of performance is acceptable and desirable for them all. Set it as a goal and write it down. School teachers need to make clear the standard of performance that is expected and accepted as achievement and what behaviors equal which scores/grades. That, too, needs to be written down. When those parameters are agreed upon, and everyone agrees on what achievement will look like, then a plan can be formulated to reach those goals.

Underachievement Busting:

Here are my four best interventions to implement to help your child break the pattern of underachievement, or not fall into it:

1. Help your child to see him/herself as a secure, competent individual as early as possible in their life. Each child needs to develop feelings of safety and being cared for and being supported and validated in their attempts to explore the world. No matter what the family background, the family issues, and what the needs and personality of the child consist of, the child has to see him/herself as an active partner in and the key to the process of success in life. No blame, no complain. What he/she DOES is going to result in his/her success or lack of it. This requires a tricky family balance of interactions as children grow older that parents don't do too much, or too little, or pass off their children's problems on other people. Underachievement begins at a very young age and is a learned behavior. As parents we have to see ourselves and how we interact with our children as part of the problem AND the solution.

2. Work together. Parents — and any other family members that work with the child — must join together to give the same clear message to the children that school and achievement are important and valued. Inattention, lack of productivity, falling behind, blaming others and aggressive/depressive behaviors are not normal or successful strategies for achievement. Parents who blame each other or the school are giving their children a message that something besides the child's own work ethic is causing

Linda Levitt

them to fail. Of course, appropriate educational practice and positive educators must be in place in a school that fits your child. (See section on Advocacy, page 89) But, conflict in the school/home team gives the child more ammunition to blame someone else, besides themselves, and continue to engage in behaviors that don't lead to achievement.

3. Get your child organized. Organization, time management, age-appropriate responsibility and setting school as a priority are skills and views that have to be developed within the child, bit by bit, starting from the first day of pre-school, and accelerated over time, no matter what it takes to do this. THIS IS NOT EASY. If you or your partner lack some of the above skill or you have conflict in teaching them, then hire someone else. (I've tried tutors, teachers, study skills programs, expensive study centers, the Homework Doctor, a friend who organizes peoples' closets for a living and my son's girlfriends.) Whoever your child will listen to and emulate, find them.

   You may have to monitor their assignment calendar, due dates, backpack, cubby or desk, and schedule until they graduate into doing this independently.

4. Demand that teachers help them. Every child can benefit from support. The ten minutes it would take each day at school to file work in notebooks, clean out back-packs and desks and check off homework is worth it.

   Find a way to monitor their organization without unnecessary intervention, criticism, and over-parenting. DON'T YOU DO IT! Just make sure it is done. You want them to learn the skills and routine.

   Make planning and organization a basic part of each day.

   It is just like making them brush their teeth—it has to be done. Without basic planning and follow-through skills, school is a disaster.

(See "Tips from the Homework Dr". in Resources)

Implementing Underachievement Busting Strategies:

1. Allow your child from the youngest age every opportunity to try things and learn from the consequences. Support them in their interests. Answer their questions. Encourage them. Let them make mistakes. Help them learn something from their mistakes. Empower them by letting them make their own choices, good and bad, within reason. Don't enable them by saving them from every consequence. Help them alter consequences by changing their behavior. Respect their points of view. Allow them to hear others' views. Learn about effective communication strategies that value your child's feelings. Don't blame, criticize and complain to your child about their behavior. Help them identify ways to change their actions and behaviors that will result in them being more successful.

2. If your child is not achieving in school, get all family members that work with your child to meet with each and every teacher WITH YOUR CHILD present, without blaming or complaining. Discuss as a team what needs to be done to fix the problem. Identify the missing behaviors.

   Is their underachievement based on inappropriate classroom behavior, poor questioning strategies, not fully listening to directions and lectures? Are their low grades based on poor test scores or missing homework?

   Go back and look at the ABC model of behavior at the beginning of this book. Make up a list of behaviors that need to change. Then look at what antecedents could be changed to alter the consequences.

Example:
Behaviors
- Child Does Not Turn In Homework
- Child Fails Chapter Tests
- Child is Disorganized and Unfocused

Linda Levitt

Behavior
Child Does Not Turn In Homework

Potential Antecedent

Teacher allows time at
lunch/recess/end of the day
to do homework and
collects it right then.

Potential Consequence

Child completes homework
gets to go to recess, has
time at home to read/study
Grades improve.

Behavior
Child Fails Chapter Tests

Potential Antecedent

Teacher calls on child
during class discussions.
Clarifies questions.
Checks to make certain
they have study materials
and books to take home.
Parents require one hour
of study time each night,
and are available to check over
work or practice skills if asked.

Potential Consequence

Child sees effort equals
a change in classroom
performance. Begins to use
needed materials for learning.
Begins to use study time at
home on strategies that may
relate to success in class.

Behavior
Child is Disorganized and Unfocused

Potential Antecedent

Teacher assigns works and helps
child get out needed materials.
Roams the room and answers
questions, redirects the child,
praises progress. Monitors work
in notebook. Parents encourage
organizing notebooks, and set aside
a study area and a time
each day for work.

Potential Consequence

Child can find needed assignment
and complete the lesson.
When parents question the
day, the child can respond
with positive statements
about their work progress.

***These three scenarios are meant to show that the child's success and achievement will be altered by the teacher's effort to help them buy into the lessons, get started, stay focused and have necessary materials at school. The parents will do the same at home by setting mandatory study time aside and by being available to help IF NEEDED. But the child will see that success and achievement was altered by the changes in their OWN behavior; paying attention, asking appropriate questions in class, keeping track of assignments and handing them in, studying correct material, keeping organized on on-track.

3. Set agreed upon and reasonable schedules and rules around the school week. At this point in our society, school is the child's primary job from age five until age 18. Encourage reading in your home as a prime activity during down time. Its value in the development of vocabulary, knowledge and interests cannot be replaced. But, since gifted children usually have other talents and interests, as well as school; sports, music, the arts, Scouts, leadership, involvement in these activities is paramount in helping your child reach their potential and find inner-fulfillment and lifelong joy. The time spent on these activities must be factored into their days.

4. If your child is disorganized, work with him! Hire someone to work with him at home! Ask the teacher to work with him until he develops a competent successful system!

No child can compete in the achievement-oriented academic world commiserate with high intelligence if they can't keep track of the necessary materials, the assignments and the required work. It starts at home, soon after birth, by not enabling your child to be lazy and disorganized. Don't pick up after them, find their shoes for them, and enable them day after day. Set aside places in your home for homework, shoes, keys and backpacks. Use them. If your child keeps losing their sweatshirt, make them go find it each day. Don't you pay for lost library books. Help them find a way to earn the money. Work with them to pick up their rooms and their stuff in a reasonable manner. Work together to create an organized study area and keep it stocked. Work with your child to have all assignments written down on an assignment calendar each week/month in whatever fashion works for you, them and their teacher.

Key Point on Underachievement Busting:
Work with your child to get assignments on a calendar, get assignments started, get them done and turned in on time.

This is easier said than done but it MUST be done. There are lots of articles on the Internet (and a great one by Victoria Olivadoti in the Resources section at the back of this book). Read them, work on this skill with your child until they master basic time management and physical organization. It is the basis for later success.

(As I continue to trip over my "piles" instead of "files" and shout at my children to find their shoes and keep track of their own cellphones and car keys, I admit that getting organized is a lot easier to write about and read about than it is to do.)

But it is imperative. No matter how funny the absent-minded relative story might seem, in this busy competitive world, lack of organization and planning can be life-threatening.

The above is the best advice I can give you. Talk to your school's administrators and teachers about organizational programs. The time you spend on helping your child get himself on the road to success is worth it. Both your futures depend on it!

Linda's CliffNotes

Linda's CliffNotes
A Summary of the Very Best Strategies for Surviving Your Terrific Kid

1. Be grateful! Smart kids are so much more fun than not-so-smart-ones. They are our future. Remember, they will be paying for our health care and trying to repair the mistakes past generations have made on this planet.

2. Be patient. Your children will grow up before you know it, and then you'll hardly ever see them. And when you do, they won't be talking to you anymore, and you'll be longing for those days when you couldn't get them to be quiet.

3. Bright children are the problem solvers of the future. Nurture their gifts and creativity. Make certain the things they really take joy in are part of their everyday lives. Be it music or baseball or computer games or animals, passion is what makes life fun. And, while they are reveling in their chosen focus, make time to find one of your own. Embrace and share yours with them.

4. Remember, the apple doesn't fall far from the tree…..if your child is so smart, you're probably pretty smart yourself. Call up your own mother or father, if you're lucky enough that they are still alive. Let them regale you with stories of how you drove them nuts at your child's age and ask them what worked or didn't work to help you be the success you are today. If your child is NOT like you…and more like your significant other…try to remember WHAT attracted you to your partner and try to celebrate what you've created with your combined DNA.

5. Listen, really listen to your child for at least 15 minutes every day, or 20 times a day if at all possible. That means listening with nothing in your hands, direct eye contact, nodding and verifying your understanding of what they are saying. Offer no advice, no commentary, no criticism. Just listen. You'll be amazed what you learn about your child and yourself. It can open the door to so many new shared interests and conversations…an enhanced relationship.

Linda Levitt

6. Work alongside your children to teach them the skills you want them to learn. Children respond better when they see you as a partner. If you want your child to learn how to do something correctly, like cursive handwriting, making the bed, planting a new rose garden, memorizing their multiplication tables or playing tennis, show them carefully and graciously as many times as necessary. Be prepared for them to argue, to improvise and attempt to improve your way! Consider a change!

7. The old adage," You learn 10% of what you see, 20% of what you hear….and something like 80% of what you teach someone else," has merit. Let your children cement their skills, expand their interests and share their talents by teaching others. They can start by teaching you and their siblings the things they are so desperate to know and to share and expand as far as their energy goes. The knowledge, ideas and power in their busy minds can change our world for the better.

8. Remember, you are the parent/grandparent or the older friend/teacher and the BOSS. Kids are smaller than you are for a reason. Be the boss if you need to be. Give them security in knowing that they can count on you to help make good decisions and keep them from blundering headlong into bad ones. Don't let them run you over. But learn to work with your children to develop reasonable guidelines and thought process in all aspects of their lives.

9. The brighter the child, the sooner they will see the chinks in your parental armor and will try to wear you down. Bright children often rebel just to see your reaction. They enjoy the power struggle. BE FIRM. " NO" is an OK answer when it fits. When parents disagree, the child will sniff out how they can take charge and usurp the power position in the family. Encourage all adults to agree on reasonable rules, guidelines, and limits within your home/homes and to consistently follow through on them.

10. Work hard to come to an agreement with your "parenting partners" about parenting styles. No matter your personal differences, the smarter the child, the quicker they will see the discrepancies and create havoc for your family….and long-range, for themselves. The child will often side with the weaker parent and turn against the disciplinarian.

11. Unstructured outdoor play and activity is one of the best things you can offer your child. However, if you live like many of us in neighborhoods and places where children can't safely roam the streets, then your guidance is essential. While they are young, encourage children to be creative, to experiment, to try new things, to strengthen their bodies and to take time to think and relax in the quiet.

12. Within reason, keep 'em busy and don't use the TV for a baby-sitter. You don't have to over-schedule your child to exhaustion with way too many lessons and structured events. But you do need to involve them with activities and people who support their interests. Research finds that the busiest kids are the most successful kids. Reading, libraries, public parks, music events, the history channel, outdoor festivals and WORK will make your child a better person. Bright but un-busy kids will often find things to do that you DON'T want them involved in. Check the percentage of kids in juvenile reform programs/drug rehabilitation centers who are considered talented or gifted. As a parent, you need to channel their energy.

13. Find and engage in activities and interests YOU are passionate about. Role model what it means to be a happy human. Your child will be more likely to do things if you do things, be it reading or gardening or collecting or sports or crossword puzzles. Be open-minded and active. Try to include your child whenever possible, or at least talk to them about your passions. Help your child find and explore any and all interests. The time you spend together driving to the zoo or gun shows or Renaissance Festivals will be well spent. Each experience enriches their lives and leads to other adventures. You are opening up doorways. As adults, they will remember and most likely replicate events and activities they saw in their childhood.

14. Don't compete with your children. Even as they get older, let them dazzle you will their knowledge and skills as often as you can. I knew a dad who felt the need to shout out the answers when the mother was quizzing their child on the multiplication tables! Good Grief! Let your child be great and clever. You don't always have to let them win, but you should be mature enough to not have to beat them at everything.

Linda Levitt

15. Accept your child for who he/she really is...no matter how difficult. Keep these words handy, "I support you on your life's path."

16. Last, but best...treat your child in the same manner as you would your most beloved friend. Talk to them quietly, honestly, kindly and often. Listen to their desires and opinions. Keep an instant replay in your mind of what you say and what you do to and with your child. Make certain it is a reflection of the very image that you want your child to keep in their memories of you for their lifetime.

Resources!

Linda Levitt

BRIGHT LEARNER VS GIFTED LEARNER

Knows the answers..Asks the questions

Is interested ....Is highly curious

Is attentive..Is involved

Has good ideas ....Has wild, silly ideas

Works hard..Plays around, yet tests well

Answers the questions ....Discusses in detail, elaborates

Top group ....Beyond the group

Listens with interest ....Shows strong feelings, opinions

Learns with ease ....Already knows

Adapted from: Janice Szabos, (1989) Bright Child, Gifted Learner. "Challenge," Good Apple.

Linda Levitt

ADD/ADHD VS GIFTEDNESS

Poor attention in most situations	Poor attention, boredom, daydreaming in specific situations
Little persistence on tasks not having immediate consequences	Little persistence on tasks that seem irrelevant
Impulsivity	Judgement lags behind intellect
More active, restless than other kids	High activity level, may need less sleep
Inappropriate unregulated social behavior	Intensity, struggles with authority
Difficulty adhering to rules and regulations	Questions rules, customs, traditions

Adapted from <u>Misdiagnosis and Dual Diagnoses of Gifted Children and Adults</u>, Webb, Amend, Webb, Goerss, Beljan, Olenchak. Great Potential Press.

Linda Levitt

GREAT NAMES FOR "GOOGLING" IDEAS AND INFORMATION ON GIFTED AND TERRIFIC CHILDREN

Armstrong, Thomas

Cohn, Sanford

Coil, Carolyn

Devries, Arlene

Galbraith, Judith

Garder, Howard

Kerr, Barbara

Kovalik, Susan

Probst, Barbara

Rimm, Sylvia

Olivadoti, Victoria

Renzulli, Joe

Reiss, Sally

Rutherford, Robert

Webb, James

Linda Levitt

WEB SITES FOR TEACHERS, FAMILIES, PARENTS AND FRIENDS OF TERRIFIC KIDS

The National Research Center on Gifted and Talented
http://www.gifted.usconn.edu/

The National Association for Gifted Children
http://www.nagc.org/

The Council For Exceptional Children
http://www.cec.sped.org/index.html

The Association for the Gifted
http://www.cectag.org

Gifted Underachieving Students
http://aegus1.org

Supporting Emotional Needs of the Gifted
http://www. SENGifted.org/

Hoagies' Gifted Education Page
http://www.hoagiesgifted.org/

Gifted-Children.com
http://www.gifted-children.com/

A Library of Blue Ribbon Learning Sites
http://www.kn.pacbell.com/wiwred/bluewebn/index.cfm

Filamentality "Learning Web:
http://www.kn.pacbell.com/wired/fil/

The Academy of Achievement
http://www.achievement.org/

Linda Levitt

ORGANIZATIONS
FOR FAMILIES AND FRIENDS OF TERRIFIC KIDS

Council for Exceptional Children (CEC)
http://www.cec

Supporting Emotional Needs of the Gifted (SENG)
http://www.SENGifted.org/

The National Association for Gifted Children (NAGC)
http://www.nagc.org/

The Association for the Education of Gifted Underachieving Students
http://www.aegus1.org

Families of the Talented and Gifted
www.TAGFAM.org

Hyperactive Children's Support Group (HACSG)
http://homepages.force9.net/hyperactive

Linda Levitt

THOMAS ARMSTRONG'S ARTICLE OF MULTIPLE INTELLIGENCES

The theory of multiple intelligences was developed in 1983 by Dr. Howard Gardner, professor of education at Harvard University. It suggests that the traditional notion of intelligence, based on I.Q. testing, is far too limited. Instead, Dr. Gardner proposes eight different intelligences to account for a broader range of human potential in children and adults. These intelligences are:

Linguistic intelligence ("word smart"):
Logical-mathematical intelligence ("number/reasoning smart")
Spatial intelligence ("picture smart")
Bodily-Kinesthetic intelligence ("body smart")
Musical intelligence ("music smart")
Interpersonal intelligence ("people smart")
Intrapersonal intelligence ("self smart")
Naturalist intelligence ("nature smart")

Dr. Gardner says that our schools and culture focus most of their attention on linguistic and logical-mathematical intelligence. We esteem the highly articulate or logical people of our culture. However, Dr. Gardner says that we should also place equal attention on individuals who show gifts in the other intelligences: the artists, architects, musicians, naturalists, designers, dancers, therapists, entrepreneurs, and others who enrich the world in which we live.

Unfortunately, many children who have these gifts don't receive much reinforcement for them in school. Many of these kids, in fact, end up being labeled "learning disabled," "ADD (attention deficit disorder,)" or simply underachievers, when their unique ways of thinking and learning aren't addressed by a heavily linguistic or logical-mathematical classroom.

The theory of multiple intelligences proposes a major transformation in the way our schools are run. It suggests that teachers be trained to present

Linda Levitt

their lessons in a wide variety of ways using music, cooperative learning, art activities, role play, multimedia, field trips, inner reflection, and much more (see Multiple Intelligences in the Classroom).

The good news is that the theory of multiple intelligences has grabbed the attention of many educators around the country, and hundreds of schools are currently using its philosophy to redesign the way it educates children. The bad new is that there are thousands of schools still out there that teach in the same old dull way, through dry lectures, and boring work-sheets and textbooks. The challenge is to get this information out to many more teachers, school administrators, and others who work with children, so that each child has the opportunity to learn in ways harmonious with their unique minds (see In Their Own Way).

Resources

Armstrong, Thomas. Multiple Intelligences in the Classroom. Alexandria, VA: Association for Supervision and Curriculum Development, 1994.

Armstrong, Thomas. 7 Kinds of Smart: Identifying and Developing Your Many Intelligences, New York: Plume, 1993.

Armstrong, Thomas. In Their Own Way: Discovering and Encouraging Your Child's Personal Learning Style, New York: Tarcher/Putnam, 1987

TIPS FROM THE HOMEWORK DR.

Victoria Olivadoti at tolivadoti.com

Homework Ailments Plaguing Homes Everywhere
Homework Doctor Has the Perfect Prescription to Cure Common Ills

Nationwide homes are plagued by homework ailments. These ailments evoke negative human responses in parents that linger on long past the completion of assignments. Have no fear, the following prescriptions will bring about quick cures for ills suffered nightly and at the same time empower your children to get their personal needs met from any teacher they may have.

Ailment #1:

I Don't know what to do Blues or the Teacher Didn't Teach Me This Blues

Cause:

Many children are accustomed to their parents re-teaching homework concepts. For this reason they do not feel a need to listen carefully in class. In order for the brain to store information for more than 2-3 seconds the child needs to feel the information is important. If a child feels no urgency to listen and pay close attention to what is being taught or reinforced, there is a strong likelihood that he/she will not know how to complete the assignment.

At home, what results is emotional upheaval and parents begin to lose confidence in the effectiveness of classroom instruction. There is a fear held by many parents that their child needs their help to succeed. Consequently, they step in and do the instruction. The child returns to school the next day with completed homework, free of errors. This leads the teacher to believe that the children fully understand the concept. As a result the teacher moves on to the next concept. The teacher is mislead to believe that the approach applied was appropriate for the children and therefore will not attempt another method to bring about understanding. Consequently, the cycle continues.

Linda Levitt

Prescription:

Parent awareness of teaching methods is very important. Educators rely heavily on student feedback. They depend on students expressing what they understand and do not understand.

When a teacher introduces a new concept, they have students apply the concept immediately to ascertain if the students have grasped the concept. It is very possible for a child to understand a concept in class, apply it right away, and yet not remember the concept once time and space has been put between the instruction and the application. Children often say they understand how to apply a concept, but they get home and realize they didn't understand it as well as they initially thought. Their first reaction is to panic and often cry that the teacher didn't teach them how to do it. They do not realize that the brain may need more exposure to the concept in order for it to reach the long-term memory and be easily retrieved and applied. The child may not have strategies to retrieve the information.

To solve this ailment, parents would better serve their children if they instruct their children how to talk to their teachers. By encouraging their children to go back to the teacher and share the need for further instruction, the child will listen differently and be more likely to remember the concept.

When a child asks a question based on a desire to understand, they are sending a message to the brain that this is important and that fact alone will improve understanding and memory retention.

Help your children determine the types of questions they might ask the teacher to help clear up understanding. For example, after initial instruction in long division, Jack came in the next morning and approached me with the following request, "when you were doing the example of long division, I was sure I understood it, but when I got home last night I forgot the steps. Will you show me how to do it again?"

Another child approached me with the following question, " I wasn't sure how to do the long division, but I tried my best. Did I do it correctly? Will you review the steps for me?"

Another child asked for more support after being instructed in the new concept of adding uncommon fractions.

If children become accustomed to asking questions about the assignment **prior** to leaving class, they will listen carefully to the answer, and consequently they will gain better understanding and have less difficulty completing the evening's assignment.

Ailment #2:
Paper Management Dysfunction Book bag Regurgitation.

Cause:

Students with this ailment do not know what to do with papers. They do not have a natural intuition for dealing with papers or do not have natural organizational skills. They may even lack motor planning skills for coping with managing materials. Pressure from parents to be neater, can cause children to shut down. They don't know how to do it differently or they would.

Prescription:

Students need a homework system that helps them organize their work in order to alleviate crumpled and lost papers. Provide a 3 ringed binder with front and back pockets that can hold an agenda. The agenda or day planner needs spaces large enough to write several assignments and after school activities. The pockets provide a perfect storage place for papers to keep them neat and tidy. The left hand pocket is designated for work to be done and the right hand pocket is designated for completed work. The agenda is a place to record each item and can be highlighted as each item is completed and placed in the completed folder.

Using visual imagery to help children plan a successful method for recording assignments and collecting the items needed to be completed for homework is very helpful for students who lack motor planning skills. This is the lack of ability to preplan a sequence of events. If students can imagine each step necessary for the successful completion of homework, they will always know where the work is, and as a result the days of wrinkled papers will end.

To help children visualize a successful homework process I use the following dialogue "To help you complete your homework successfully I want

Linda Levitt

you to see yourself being successful. So close your eyes and see yourself coming into the classroom and taking out your homework notebook. Can you see yourself doing this?" I continue by stating, "See yourself looking at the board to see the homework assignment. Can you see that? Now see yourself recording the assignment in the agenda. Can you see yourself writing in your agenda? I'd like you to see yourself collecting your materials needed to be successful? Can you see yourself doing that? Now look at the worksheet and read it as if you are going to do it right away. Can you see yourself doing this?

"Now I would like you to ask questions about anything that is unclear. Can you see yourself asking for clarification? Now you know how to do all parts of your homework, see yourself putting it in the front pocket of your agenda. See yourself placing the folder in your backpack along with any books or supplies you need. Now take that book bag home and take out the folder. See yourself numbering the items in the order you would like to complete them. I suggest doing the hardest ones first and getting it out of the way. Can you see yourself doing this?

"Now take the first item out of the front pocket and complete it. Place it in the back pocket and highlight that time off on your agenda. Now do the same thing for the remaining items. Can you see yourself doing this? The next step is to look at the agenda and be sure that you have completed and highlighted all assignments. Are they complete? Place them in your backpack and place your backpack by the door from which you will leave the next day. Place it in a position that will require you to move it when you leave the house the next day. Can you see yourself doing this? Now pat yourself on the back because you have been successful."

Being empathetic about the difficulty your child might be having regarding organization will help. Children who lack organizational skills need to be aware that this is just one area where they need to concentrate. When they first began to kick a ball, they didn't do it without focusing really hard on the ball. Once they practiced and concentrated, they eventually began to kick the ball naturally. The same is true for tracking their papers. In the beginning, they need to pay deliberate attention to the papers they must manage. This situation will always require focused attention. Being aware that they need to use focused attention and that nothing is wrong with them will often relieve the stress they feel connected to managing papers and make the job of organizing less taxing.

If children have trouble visualizing the situation, they may be auditory learners and can remember the process by hearing you say the method. In their situation I will ask them to hear me describing the pattern. One student informed me that she pushes a button behind her ear and replays my script, and therefore she can remember the steps. Children often do not realize that they are capable of creating visual imagery since they are so conditioned to receiving images created for them. I ask these children to think back to what they did this summer. If they can see themselves doing an activity, they will be able to us visualization as a support system for managing homework.

Ailment 3:
Minute Minder Deficient- Last Minute Sweats
Sufferers of Procrastination

Cause:

Children have a poor concept of time. To many children it seems like an eternity between December 1st and December 25th, so it stands to reason that the project assigned a month earlier can creep up on them. Children have difficulty understanding what 15 minutes feels like so it is makes sense that they run out of time when they are asked to do a long-term project. Once the due date creeps up on them they do not have a plan to deal with it. Some teachers provide deadlines for different parts of assignments, yet they have no meaning to the student.

Some students share that their parents plan activities after school or on weekends that they don't know about and therefore cannot plan for them.

A major reason for procrastination is the activity is difficult or they are not good at the subject, so they put it off as long as possible. Without a plan for dealing with the difficulties, students wait until the last minute, and are often rescued by their parents, so they never learn how to plan effectively.

Linda Levitt

Prescription

   If we want our children to be able to plan effectively they need to be included in the scheduling and informed of family responsibilities well in advance.

   We can help children develop a sense of time. When children are young, refer to activities in terms of how much time they take. When traveling from one destination to another define the distance in miles and time.

   We want children to understand what fifteen minutes feel like before we can teach them to plan for a week-long or month-long project. Using a daily schedule to give them a feel for time is helpful. Introduce a daily schedule for each day of the week that is divided into fifteen-minute increments. Have children list all the activities that need to be done during the week and assess how much time they think they will need to complete them.

   Allowing children to determine how much each activity will take for themselves might be surprising. Some children will need twenty minutes to get dressed while others only require five minutes. The planning needs to include all after school activities. Place these activities on the lines that correspond to the time they will be taking place. Students fail to allow for dressing time, time for finding their clothes, and travel time for their extracurricular activities. Encourage children to allow for these activities.

   Using a highlighter, they are to highlight any time that is not available for homework. Once they highlight the time devoted to sports activities, dinner, chores, preparing for bed and bedtime, it becomes very clear how little time is available to complete homework.

   The typical procrastinator completes assignments at the last minute. The highlighting creates a visual so they can see that they don't have the time they once thought they had available to them to complete an assignment.

   The children are then expected to fill in the specific homework assignments in the white spaces remaining. Allow children to decide when and where they will complete their assignments. By doing so they have a vested interest in their choices and will use their time more effectively.

   Once this activity is completed, it becomes internalized and they easily recognize how little time they may possess. It will not be necessary to do this activity for more than one week. It is incredibly powerful.

Help your children develop a sense of elapsed time by suggesting they record the beginning and the ending time they spend on an assignment.

Children will plan better if they recognize that they have other options should their evenings be overscheduled. Suggesting that they utilize some of their free time during the school day to get started on their work will help them compensate for lack of after school time. This concept is something many students don't think about. They can opt to get started on their homework during recess or at lunch. Others will utilize their study hall time for work completion rather than for socializing.

The evening is a good time to evaluate the effectiveness of that day's scheduling and for creating a plan for change if necessary.

Many children are working under the misconception that they are expected to be good at everything. When they face a subject that does not come easily, they tend to avoid doing it. If children are avoiding the activity because it is difficult, a little demystification is very helpful. Helping them recognize that they are avoiding the activity because it is difficult and letting them know it is okay to not be good at everything will be reassuring. "I know this is difficult for you. Just think of how much better you will feel if you just get it out of the way."

Children can recognize the benefit of working at a subject until they improve when you compare it how they performed when they began a new sport. They weren't very good at first. How did they get better? They practiced. In the same way, their performance in a hard subject will improve if they give it a little more effort. If this is the reason they are avoiding the work, often sharing this analogy, coupled with the daily planner will result in an improvement in time management.

Backwards Planning puts time in perspective and personalizes a month long project for students. It uses students' internal clocks when planning for project completion. Students working on long-term projects are asked to think of the last thing they will be doing to complete the project. They make a list of each of the activities working backwards.

The next step is to determine how many days each part of the project will take them. Working backwards creates a sense of urgency to get started

135   Linda Levitt

right away. If teachers provide due dates, students still need to plan backwards as their personal time clocks may require more time than the teacher has allowed.

Since students don't often think of all the obstacles that could befall them, encouraging them to allow for computer crashes, disk failures, and lack of ink in the computer by back dating the due date will assure them of success and cure the "Last Minute Sweats"

Understand the common complaints of students and appropriate responses for 40 of the most common homework challenges available in <u>Homework Solutions for the Weary Student and Their Parents</u> through amazon.com or by contacting Victoria Olivadoti at tolivadoti.com.

Reprinted with permission from The Homework Dr.
Victoria Olivadoti.

REMEMBER...

HOW TO RUIN YOUR TERRIFIC CHILD
IN TWELVE EASY STEPS

1. ALWAYS have to be right. Make certain your child knows YOU are much smarter than they are.

2. Stay in CONTROL of your child's life as much as you possible can! Boss them around! Save them from every mistakes or incorrect decision!

3. CRITICIZE your child at every possible opportunity – their hair, clothes, grades, friends, ideas, interests!

4. Expect your child to be PERFECT! Never settle for SECOND BEST!

5. Make sure your child knows THEIR BEHAVIOR EMBARRASSES you and the family. Tell them often and in front of other people

6. Fill your home with conflict and disagreement over parenting and child-rearing practices.

7. Expect order, organization and cleanliness from your child at all times.

8. Don't praise your child. It might spoil them.

9. Hang on to every word your child utters. Photograph every move. Make certain your child's every wish and demand is met.

10. TV, video games and computers make great baby-sitters. Sit your child in front of one as often as possible.

11. Say "SHHH" and "BE QUIET" a hundred times a day.

12. Use the phrase "BECAUSE I SAID SO" as your primary form of decision-making.

Linda Levitt

About the Author

Linda Levitt holds both a B.A. and M.A. in Special Education from Arizona State University with an interest and emphasis in Behavior Management. She is a veteran of thirty years of classroom teaching, specializing in gifted education. Her personal stories appear in LifeLines: Stories of Love, Life, Loss, Family and Hope (AppleStar Publishing). Through her newest venture, Educating Exceptional Learners, Linda consults with families and school districts. She supervises teachers for Arizona State University, sits on the board of directors for Scottsdale Supporters of the Gifted, and manages the nonprofit organization, Environmental Connections.

Linda is a writing member of Sisters on the Fly, Baby Boomer Women, the National Association of Women Writers, and MommyTalk.com. She is married, raising two sons, two step-daughters, and two dogs in Paradise Valley, Arizona.

Dynamic Titles Available From NL Associates Inc.

Not Just Schoolwork

Write, From the Beginning
(Revised Edition)

Thinking and Writing Activities for the Brain! Books 1 and 2

Creativity Day-by-Day (Stimulating Activities for Kids and Adults)

Stories with Holes Volumes 1-20

Intriguing Questions Volumes 1-6

Whose Clues Volumes 1-6

*Nathan Levy's Test Booklet of Basic Knowledge
for Every American Over 9 Years Old*

There Are Those

101 Things Everyone Should Know About Science

What To Do When Your Kid is Smarter Than You
by Linda Levitt

Above titles written by Nathan Levy, unless otherwise noted.

Please contact us to receive workshop and/or ordering information.
NL Associates, Inc.
P.O. Box 1199
Hightstown, NJ 08520-0399
(732) 605-1643
www.storieswithholes.com